PreScripts

Cursive Sentences and Art Lessons

Medieval to Modern World History

CLASSICALCONVERSATIONS.COM

PreScripts Cursive Sentences and Art Lessons: Medieval to Modern World History

Created by Courtney Sanford and Jennifer Greenholt
Illustrations by Kelly Digges

©2013 by Classical Conversations® MultiMedia
All rights reserved.
No part of this publication may be reproduced, stored in a retrieval system, or transmitted in any form or by any means—electronic, mechanical, photocopy, recording, or any other—without the prior permission of the publisher, except as follows: permission is granted for copies of reproducible pages to be made for use within your own family.

Published in the U.S.A. by Classical Conversations, Inc.
P.O. Box 909
West End, NC 27376

ISBN: 978-0-9884965-2-1

For ordering information, visit www.ClassicalConversationsBooks.com.
Printed in the United States of America

Table of Contents

A Note for Parents 6

Forming the Cursive Letters 8

Using a Grid 10

Using Mapping to Draw 11

History Sentences and Drawing Lessons 1–6..12

    Review Lessons 1–6..36

History Sentences and Drawing Lessons 7–12..44

    Review Lessons 7–12..68

History Sentences and Drawing Lessons 13–18..76

    Review Lessons 13–18.. 100

History Sentences and Drawing Lessons 19–24.. 108

    Review Lessons 19–24.. 132

A Note for Parents: Tools for the Journey

Introduction

The word "prescript" comes from the Latin words *prae* (meaning "before" or "in front of") plus *scribere* (meaning "to write"). The PreScripts series from Classical Conversations MultiMedia is designed to precede—to come before—writing. Just as we learn to speak by mimicking our parents' words, we can learn to write well by copying the words that others have written. Even though coloring, drawing, tracing, and copying are simple tasks from an adult perspective, imitation is at the heart of a classical education. In order to learn how to write, children must first acquire fine motor skills and learn to sit still and follow instructions. They do so with the help of simple tasks like these. Rather than resorting to mindless busywork that isolates our youngest children from their family's education, the PreScripts series is designed to initiate young learners into the world of knowledge they will inhabit as they mature.

Each book in the PreScripts series combines a functional design with excellent content. The goal of *PreScripts Cursive Sentences and Art Lessons* is to take the building blocks of cursive writing (letters, words, and simple sentences) and funnel them into longer sentences and more writing practice. As they gain confidence and skill, your students will first trace each sentence and then write it, keeping the model nearby.

Our job as classical educators is to teach students to make the effort to be neat, but preferably to aim higher by teaching them to write beautifully. Many schools no longer teach cursive writing, claiming that it is too difficult for young children to master. Teaching a child to write in cursive does require diligence and patience, but it has a number of compelling benefits. Research suggests that cursive writing more effectively develops manual skill and dexterity. Cursive may also aid students struggling with dyslexia or dysgraphia because (1) capital and lowercase letters are distinct; (2) each word is one fluid movement, so the child's rhythm is not disrupted by frequent pauses; and (3) letters like "b" and "d" are more difficult to reverse.

While they master the manual skill of writing, students will also reinforce writing and reading rules. They will begin to notice unusual punctuation—for example, hyphenated words at the end of a line or an ellipsis […] to show that part of a quote has been eliminated—and will be less likely to stumble when they encounter these practices in other books. When your child becomes curious, take a moment to explain these rules. As a result, writing correctly will come more naturally to them when they compose their own sentences.

How to Use This Book

When children are learning to read and write, the 'what' matters as much as the 'how.' Parents are more likely to give up on cursive when the content seems frivolous, so Classical Conversations is pleased to offer cursive writing books that give the student plenty of practice using rich, meaningful content. With PreScripts cursive writing books, your student can become a confident writer while learning or reviewing important subject matter, such as history sentences, passages of literature, and proverbs.

In this book, students will copy sentences about medieval and world history. The book is divided into four sets of six history notes each, so upon completion, your child will have had the opportunity to master twenty-four history notes about Charlemagne, the Magna Carta, and the Hundred Years' War, among other topics. After every set, we have included a review section to ensure that your child not only masters the cursive letters and words but also retains the historical content.

To provide some variety for your child, drawing lessons are sprinkled throughout the book. Drawing will also help children develop the fine motor skills necessary for writing and provide practice in working independently. This book focuses on elements of design and composition, such as depth, point of view, and light and shadow.

Your child will enjoy experimenting with different drawing techniques, such as grids and mapping. A basic pencil and eraser will be sufficient to complete these drawing lessons, but you may find it helpful to have a soft pencil (HB or 2B) and a hard pencil (2H), as well as a blending stump and a soft Art Gum eraser. The exercises are simple enough for your child to do independently and will appeal to different senses and learning styles while continuing to reinforce the content of the history sentences.

Although variety is important, the key to mastering cursive is to practice every day. For best results, set aside a specific time each day for cursive practice. You choose the pace appropriate for your child. You can assign one page a day to a beginning student or assign two to four pages a day to an older or more experienced student. A very young student, or one who struggles with writing, might even do half a page a day until his or her fine motor skills become stronger, working up to a page or two a day. The pace is completely up to the parent.

If you choose to do one page a day, you should have enough pages for a complete school year, completing approximately four or five pages a week. If you participate in a Classical Conversations community, you can do four pages a week while your community meets and five pages a week the rest of the school year. Older children might do two pages a day and complete two books a year. If you would like your child to memorize the history sentences in this book, you can read through the sentences weekly to review or have your student do the same book twice. The second time through, have your student write the sentences into a notebook and draw in a sketch book.

The Journey in Perspective

The key to good writing is daily practice. The key to a heart that seeks truth, beauty, and goodness is providing quality content to copy. We hope you will find both in *Prescripts Cursive Sentences and Art Lessons*.

The goal of the PreScripts series is for children to master the skills of copying and writing in the context of a biblical worldview, building on a second meaning of the word "prescript." A prescript can also mean a command, rule, or moral guideline. The Bible instructs parents to remember the commandments of God and teach them to their children.

Deuteronomy 6:6–9 (NIV) reads, "And these words which I command you today shall be in your heart. You shall teach them diligently to your children, and shall talk of them when you sit in your house, when you walk by the way, when you lie down, and when you rise up. You shall bind them as a sign on your hand, and they shall be as frontlets between your eyes. You shall write them on the doorposts of your house and on your gates." As this Scripture reminds us, writing, memorizing, and reciting are all forms of worship that we model for our children.

Let's get started!

Forming the Cursive Letters

Trace, then write each letter.

Using a Grid

Detail of a miniature of Charlemagne being crowned emperor

One way that artists draw from a picture is to use a **grid**. Draw three lines across and three lines down on the original drawing to make your grid.

On your drawing paper, draw three* lines across and three lines down to form a blank grid. Use a hard pencil, which will make a light line.

To draw, just look at one square at a time and draw exactly what you see in that square. Fill in all your squares to match the squares of the original. Draw lightly at first so you can easily redraw a line with a darker pencil.

This method will help you get the basic lines in the right place for your drawing. Use a softer pencil to add the details to your drawing. Erase the grid lines to complete your drawing.

*You do not have to use three lines. You can use more if the drawing is very detailed.

Using Mapping to Draw

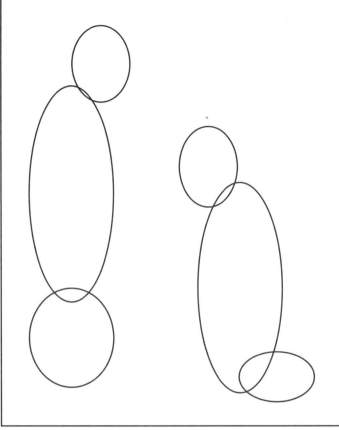

Another way to start a sketch is to **map** what you will be drawing. This means to lightly draw "blobs" of similar shape and size compared to the main shapes in a drawing. Then, the artist draws in a more detailed shape.

The blobs are a guide to help you keep all the elements of your drawing the right size and in the right place. It works just like a map, highlighting the general shapes you will use.

Be sure to draw lightly (with a hard pencil if you have one) so that you can erase the guidelines later. Use a softer pencil to draw in the contour lines (the actual outlines or edges of the elements of the drawing).

In the art lessons that follow, you will be asked to draw some illustrations. You can choose either a grid or mapping to start drawing your illustration.

Each illustration relates to a card from the *Classical Acts & Facts History Card* Timeline. If you have these cards, you might want to look at them while you draw. It may give you more details or ideas for coloring the finished drawing with colored pencils.

Detail of a miniature of Charlemagne being crowned emperor

History Note 1(a) Trace, then write the sentence.

In 800 A.D., during the medieval period,

Pope Leo III crowned Charlemagne Holy Roman

Emperor of Europe.

History Note 1(b) Trace, then write the sentence.

In 800 A.D. during the medieval period,

Pope Leo III crowned Charlemagne Holy Roman

Emperor of Europe.

Pattern

Detail of a miniature of Charlemagne being crowned emperor

This is a drawing of Charlemagne being crowned Holy Roman Emperor. There is a pattern on the wall behind the two men. An artist creates a **pattern** by repeating an element. Here, lines are repeated across and down. You can also see a pattern on the tablecloth made of curves and short lines.

Patterns are all around you. You might see them on wallpaper, carpets, dishes, or even your own clothes.

To create a pattern in your own artwork, choose an element to repeat: a line, shape, or color. Then repeat it across and down to fill an area. To see if you have created a pattern, ask yourself, "Can I tell what comes next?" If there is enough repetition that you know what will come next, it is a pattern!

Draw this composition in the space below, including the pattern in the background. Or, draw your own composition, including a pattern in the background or on a tablecloth or clothing.

Remember to choose either a grid or mapping to help you get started.

Your drawing:

History Note 2(a) Trace, then write the sentence.

After the church split into Roman Catholic and Eastern Orthodox, William the Conqueror defeated King Harold of England in 1066 and started feudalism.

History Note 2(b) Trace, then write the sentence.

After the church split into Roman Catholic and Eastern Orthodox, William the Conqueror defeated King Harold of England in 1066 and started feudalism.

Architecture Styles

Eastern-Orthodox cupola, Russia

Basilica roof, Florence, Italy

This illustration shows an Eastern Orthodox Church in Russia on the left and a Roman Catholic Church in Italy on the right.

The dome on the left is called an onion dome because it looks like an onion. Its shape might remind you of a candle flame, too. Sometimes, architects arrange three of these onion domes together to represent God the Father, Son, and Holy Spirit.

The church on the right does not have quite the same shape. It is sometimes called a helmet dome. Does it remind you of an ancient soldier's helmet?

Both designs are good for snowy areas because the snow slides right off instead of building up and getting so heavy it might collapse the roof. They also both point to heaven, reminding everyone to turn their eyes to God.

What other similarities or differences do you notice between the two styles?

Try drawing both types of domes in the space below.

Your drawing:

History Note 3(a) Trace, then write the sentence.

Eleanor of Aquitaine and her son, Richard the Lion-Hearted, fought the Turks for Jerusalem during the time of the Crusades, which occurred from 1095 to 1291.

History Note 3(b) Trace, then write the sentence.

Eleanor of Aquitaine and her son, Richard the Lion-Hearted, fought the Turks for Jerusalem during the time of the Crusades, which occurred from 1095 to 1291.

Elements of Composition

The Nándorfehérvár Battle

This drawing tells the story of a battle during the Crusades. The artist captured many things that happened during the battle.

Elements are arranged in the space so that some things are happening in the front, near the viewer. The central figure is a warrior just about to strike his enemy. This front area is called the **foreground**.

A little further back, you see the priest with his arm raised. This area is called the **middle ground**. There are other struggles going on in the middle ground. Can you find them?

The **background** of this composition consists of a horizontal line, which is the line where the earth meets the sky. In this case, it is a jagged line, creating some hills. Also, the sky is an important part of the background.

Try drawing a composition like this one in which you have figures in the foreground, some figures in the middle ground, and something in the background.

Your drawing:

History Note 4(a) Trace, then write the sentence.

English King John signed the Magna Carta in 1215, limiting the king's power. Later, England's King Edward III claimed to be king of France and began the Hundred Years' War in 1337.

History Note 4(b) Trace, then write the sentence.

English King John signed the Magna Carta in 1215,

limiting the king's power. Later, England's King

Edward III claimed to be king of France and

began the Hundred Years' War in 1337.

Depth

King John signs the Magna Carta

The document on the table, England's Magna Carta, takes the center spot in this composition. There is only a little action in this drawing: King John, on the right, signing his name. Everyone else is standing still and looking at the paper.

The artist drew very small men in the background to create **depth,** which is the illusion that you are not just looking at a flat paper, but that you are looking at something with three dimensions. In this case, it is a scene that goes back for quite a distance.

When elements that are normally about the same size (for example, the humans in this picture) are drawn in different sizes, the larger ones appear to be closer than the smaller ones.

Do you see the tiny trees in the background? Since you know trees are normally very large, your brain tells you that since they are drawn small, they must be far away.

Try drawing this composition, or a similar one, in which you create depth by drawing large objects in the foreground and small objects in the background.

Your drawing:

History Note 5(a) Trace, then write the sentence.

During the Hundred Years' War, Joan of Arc and King Charles VII led the French to defeat England at the Battle of Orleans. In the late 1340s, fleas on rats carried the Plague, which killed one out of three Europeans.

History Note 5(b) Trace, then write the sentence.

During the Hundred Years' War, Joan of Arc and King Charles VII led the French to defeat England at the Battle of Orleans. In the late 1340s, fleas on rats carried the Plague, which killed one out of three Europeans.

Drawing a Human Figure

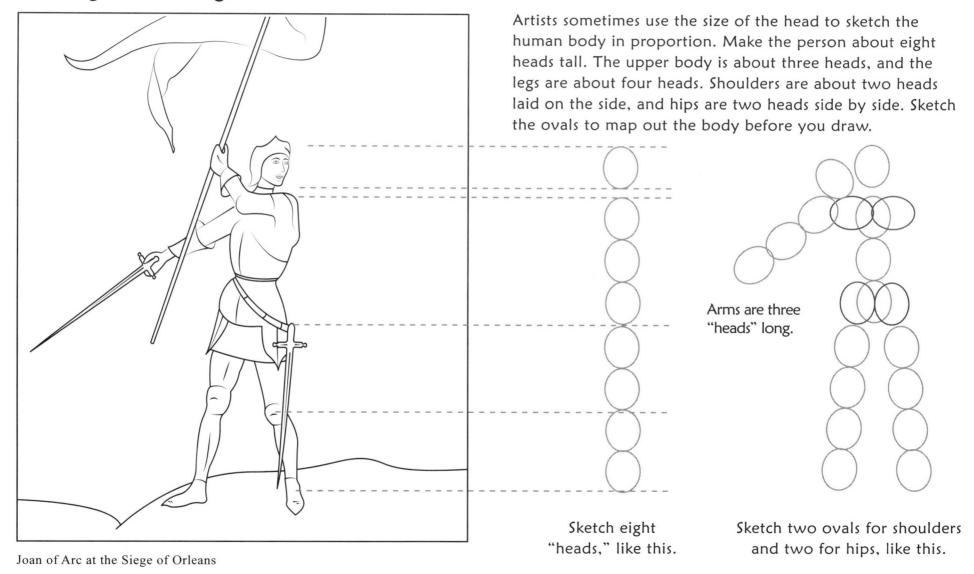

Artists sometimes use the size of the head to sketch the human body in proportion. Make the person about eight heads tall. The upper body is about three heads, and the legs are about four heads. Shoulders are about two heads laid on the side, and hips are two heads side by side. Sketch the ovals to map out the body before you draw.

Arms are three "heads" long.

Sketch eight "heads," like this.

Sketch two ovals for shoulders and two for hips, like this.

Joan of Arc at the Siege of Orleans

Map out Joan of Arc using ovals as shown here, then draw in the details.

Your drawing:

History Note 6(a) Trace, then write the sentence.

During the Renaissance period, from 1350 to 1600,

da Vinci was a famous inventor. Shakespeare was

a famous playwright. Michelangelo was a famous

artist, and Copernicus was a famous scientist.

History Note 6(b) Trace, then write the sentence.

During the Renaissance period, from 1350 to 1600,

da Vinci was a famous inventor. Shakespeare was

a famous playwright. Michelangelo was a famous

artist, and Copernicus was a famous scientist.

Design a Flying Machine

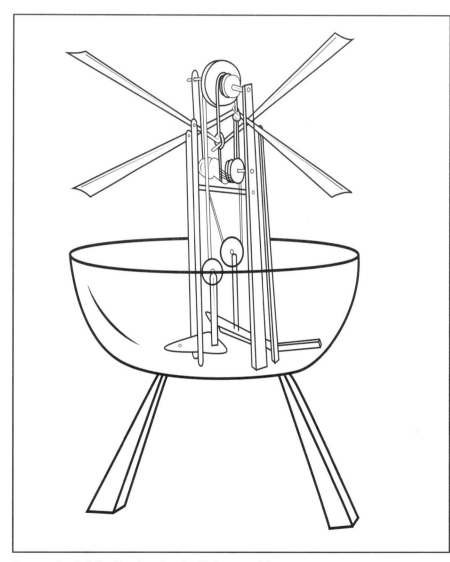

Leonardo da Vinci's sketch of a flying machine

Leonardo da Vinci was a famous artist who studied painting and sculpture as an apprentice. He is famous for painting the *Mona Lisa* and *The Last Supper*.

He also studied the human body and plants. He designed buildings, weapons, and even a robotic arm. A person like da Vinci is sometimes called a "Renaissance Man," which refers to a person who has wide interests and is an expert in many subjects.

This drawing is from one of da Vinci's sketchbooks. It is an idea for a flying machine.

Try drawing da Vinci's flying machine, or design your own in the space below. Consider becoming a "Renaissance man" (or woman) yourself and learn about lots of subjects!

Your drawing:

History Note 1(c) Review. Trace, then write the sentence.

In 800 A.D. during the medieval period,

Pope Leo III crowned Charlemagne Holy

Roman Emperor of Europe.

History Note 2(c) Review. Trace, then write the sentence.

After the church split into Roman Catholic and Eastern Orthodox, William the Conqueror defeated King Harold of England in 1066 and started feudalism.

History Note 3(c) Review. Trace, then write the sentence.

Eleanor of Aquitaine and her son, Richard the Lion-Hearted, fought the Turks for Jerusalem during the time of the Crusades, which occurred from 1095 to 1291.

For practice, draw one of the art lessons again in this space.

History Note 4(c) Review. Trace, then write the sentence.

English King John signed the Magna Carta in 1215, limiting the king's power. Later, England's King Edward III claimed to be king of France and began the Hundred Years' War in 1337.

History Note 5(c) Review. Trace, then write the sentence.

During the Hundred Years' War, Joan of Arc and King Charles VII led the French to defeat England at the Battle of Orleans. In the late 1340s, fleas on rats carried the Plague, which killed one out of three Europeans.

History Note 6(c) Review. Trace, then write the sentence.

During the Renaissance period, from 1350 to 1600, da Vinci was a famous inventor. Shakespeare was a famous playwright. Michelangelo was a famous artist, and Copernicus was a famous scientist.

For practice, draw one of the art lessons again in this space.

History Note 7(a) Trace, then write the sentence.

In 1517, Martin Luther began the Protestant Reformation by printing the Ninety-five Theses that made Pope Leo X excommunicate him. Later, John Calvin joined the Reformation.

History Note 7(b) Trace, then write the sentence.

In 1517, Martin Luther began the Protestant Reformation by printing the Ninety-five Theses that made Pope Leo X excommunicate him. Later, John Calvin joined the Reformation.

Manuscript Illuminations

Detail from New Testament translation by Luther (woodcut)

o you see a large letter D in this drawing? Before the printing press was invented, books were copied by hand. The person copying the book had to be quite an artist to copy the text perfectly and neatly. He also added illustrations and **illuminations**, like this letter D where the first letter of the first sentence was drawn very ornately and much larger than the other letters. Many manuscripts were also painted, and sometimes the artists even applied real gold to the images.

Try drawing this beautiful D in the space below, or try illustrating the first letter of your name, adding elements to it that describe the things you like.

You may want to try writing a paragraph that starts with your letter so you can see how it looks with the text wrapped around it, as it is in the paragraph above.

Your drawing:

History Note 8(a) Trace, then write the sentence.

Between the late 1400s and the mid-1500s, Dias rounded the Cape of Good Hope. Amerigo Vespucci sailed to the Americas. Balboa crossed Central America to the Pacific. Magellan's crew sailed around the globe, and Coronado explored the American Southwest.

History Note 8(b) Trace, then write the sentence.

Between the late 1400s and the mid-1500s, Dias rounded the Cape of Good Hope, Amerigo Vespucci sailed to the Americas, Balboa crossed Central America to the Pacific, Magellan's crew sailed around the globe, and Coronado explored the American Southwest.

Point of View

Spanish Conquistadors in the Americas

You have to look closely at this illustration to see that the artist chose an interesting **point of view**: the artist seems to have positioned himself below and to the side of the cross. Can you see the wooden cross? It is barely in the picture, but if you look closely, you will see it.

Placing the viewer low and near the cross makes it feel like we are in the picture with the soldiers. Perhaps the artist is inviting us to participate.

Try drawing this compostion and while you do, imagine you are right in there with the soldiers as they lay their weapons down and confess their sins.

Your drawing:

History Note 9(a) Trace, then write the sentence.

Between the 1500s and 1700s, Henry VIII of England,

Louis XIV of France, Philip II of Spain, Peter the

Great of Russia, and Frederick the Great of Prussia

ruled during the age of absolute monarchs.

History Note 9(b) Trace, then write the sentence.

Between the 1500s and 1700s, Henry VIII of England,
Louis XIV of France, Philip II of Spain, Peter the
Great of Russia, and Frederick the Great of Prussia
ruled during the age of absolute monarchs.

Art for Kings

Imperial Crown of Austria

The crown you see here was worn by the kings of Austria. It is made of gold and many precious stones. The purpose of the crown was to make the wearer look powerful and impressive.

The artist arranged the stones in patterns. There is a pattern around the bottom edge. Can you find that pattern?

Often crowns were so heavy that the wearers got headaches when they wore them. But the royals were probably more concerned with looking important than being comfortable.

Try drawing this crown in the space below, or design your own crown using some patterns.

Your drawing:

History Note 10(a) Trace, then write the sentence.

Vladimir I brought Christianity to Russia in the 900s. In the late 1400s, Czar Ivan the Great built the Kremlin in Moscow. Catherine the Great expanded and westernized Russia in the late 1700s.

History Note 10(b) Trace, then write the sentence.

Vladimir I brought Christianity to Russia in the 900s. In the late 1400s, Czar Ivan the Great built the Kremlin in Moscow. Catherine the Great expanded and westernized Russia in the late 1700s.

The Rule of Thirds

Detail from *Ivan the Great Tearing the Khan's Letter to Pieces*

Sometimes artists put the main figure in the center of a composition, but at other times artists will use the **rule of thirds**.

If you divide a picture into thirds across and down you will have this kind of a grid over the picture:

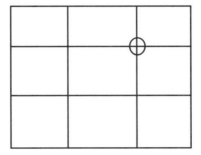

The four points where the lines cross make good places to put the main character of a composition. In the drawing at the left, Ivan's face is not in the center. It is positioned where two lines of the grid cross. (It is marked with an O in the grid above.)

Placing your main character on one of these four points will make a more interesting composition.

Try drawing Ivan, or your own composition, using the rule of thirds.

Your drawing:

History Note 11(a) Trace, then write the sentence.

In 1789, the French Revolution began when citizens stormed the Bastille and fought for the Declaration of the Rights of Man. Later, during the Reign of Terror, the aristocrats' heads were removed by the guillotine.

History Note 11(b) Trace, then write the sentence.

In 1789, the French Revolution began when citizens stormed the Bastille and fought for the Declaration of the Rights of Man. Later, during the Reign of Terror, the aristocrats' heads were removed by the guillotine.

Shadows

Detail from *An Execution, Place de la Revolution*

Light is a very important part of any piece of art. The artist decides where the light is coming from and then fills in the areas that are in the shade and highlights areas that are hit with rays of light.

Light can also tell you what time of day it is. At noon, the sun is directly over head, which makes the shadows small. Early in the morning or late in the evening, the sun is low on the horizon, which makes shadows long.

In this drawing, can you see the dog's shadow? It is long, so we know that this is a moment in the late afternoon or early morning.

Try drawing the dog and his shadow. If you have a blending tool, you can smudge the shadow to make it look a little fuzzy. You can even use your finger to smudge it a little.

Experiment with different sizes of shadows until you feel like you can tell the time of day in your drawings.

Your drawing:

History Note 12(a) Trace, then write the sentence.

Napoleon Bonaparte of the French Empire was

defeated at the Battle of Waterloo by British

General Wellington soon after the War of 1812 in

the United States.

History Note 12(b) Trace, then write the sentence.

Napoleon Bonaparte of the French Empire was defeated at the Battle of Waterloo by British General Wellington soon after the War of 1812 in the United States.

Symbolism

Detail of *Napoleon I On His Imperial Throne*

In this portrait of Napoleon, you can see that the artist decided to center Napoleon in the composition. This makes a very formal, serious portrait. If you look at all the details, you can learn a lot about Napoleon because the artist included items that tell us more about the person. These items are **symbols**.

Napoleon is wearing a crown like the ancient Greeks wore, symbolizing intelligence and power. The fine clothing and the throne also tell us that he is king-like. Napoleon was not king because he was born a prince; he was "emperor" because he proclaimed himself to be one. He had this painting made to back up his claim to the throne.

Another detail is the way the throne makes an arc behind Napoleon's head. This is similar to the way artists paint light shining behind the head of Jesus or the angels. This is supposed to make Napoleon look even more important than a regular king!

One other detail you might notice is that there is a pillow under his feet. This is because Napoleon was so short his feet did not touch the floor.

Draw Napoleon, or draw a portrait of yourself wearing and holding special things that tell us about you. For example, if you love to play soccer, draw yourself wearing your uniform and holding a soccer ball.

Your drawing:

History Note 7(c) Review. Trace, then write the sentence.

In 1517, Martin Luther began the Protestant Reformation by printing the Ninety-five Theses that made Pope Leo X excommunicate him. Later, John Calvin joined the Reformation.

History Note 8(c) Review. Trace, then write the sentence.

Between the late 1400s and the mid-1500s, Dias rounded the Cape of Good Hope, Amerigo Vespucci sailed to the Americas, Balboa crossed Central America to the Pacific, Magellan's crew sailed around the globe, and Coronado explored the American Southwest.

History Note 9(c) Review. Trace, then write the sentence.

Between the 1500s and 1700s, Henry VIII of England,

Louis XIV of France, Philip II of Spain, Peter the

Great of Russia, and Frederick the Great of Prussia

ruled during the age of absolute monarchs.

For practice, draw one of the art lessons again in this space.

History Note 10(c) Review. Trace, then write the sentence.

Vladimir I brought Christianity to Russia in the 900s. In the late 1400s, Czar Ivan the Great built the Kremlin in Moscow. Catherine the Great expanded and westernized Russia in the late 1700s.

History Note 11(c) Review. Trace, then write the sentence.

In 1789, the French Revolution began when citizens stormed the Bastille and fought for the Declaration of the Rights of Man. Later, during the Reign of Terror, the aristocrats' heads were removed by the guillotine.

History Sentence 12(c) Review. Trace, then write the sentence.

Napoleon Bonaparte of the French Empire was defeated at the Battle of Waterloo by British General Wellington soon after the War of 1812 in the United States.

For practice, draw one of the art lessons again in this space.

History Note 13(a) Trace, then write the sentence.

Watt's steam engine, Cartwright's power loom, and Whitney's cotton gin spurred the Industrial Revolution that began in the 1760s.

History Note 13(b) Trace, then write the sentence.

Watt's steam engine, Cartwright's power loom, and Whitney's cotton gin spurred the Industrial Revolution that began in the 1760s.

Technical Drawing

Steam Locomotive

Some artists specialize in **technical drawings**. In these types of drawings, the artist includes as much detail as possible, which will help construct the building or invention. In this illustration, the technical drawing is of a steam locomotive. In this type of illustration, the artist only draws one side straight on. This helps everyone working on the project know where things go and how they connect.

Try drawing this steam engine. Use a ruler for all the straight lines. Using a very sharp pencil will help keep your lines straight and smooth. You might even want to use a compass to draw perfectly round wheels. Technical drawing is very precise, but you can still start with a grid or map lines to help you place the drawing on the paper. Just be sure to erase them carefully when you are finished.

Your drawing:

History Note 14(a) Trace, then write the sentence.

Clemenceau of France, Lloyd George of England,

Nicholas II of Russia, Wilhelm II of Germany, and

Wilson of the U.S. were leaders during World War I,

which started in 1914 and ended in 1918.

History Note 14(b) Trace, then write the sentence.

Clemenceau of France, Lloyd George of England,

Nicholas II of Russia, Wilhelm II of Germany, and

Wilson of the U.S. were leaders during World War I,

which started in 1914 and ended in 1918.

Map of Europe

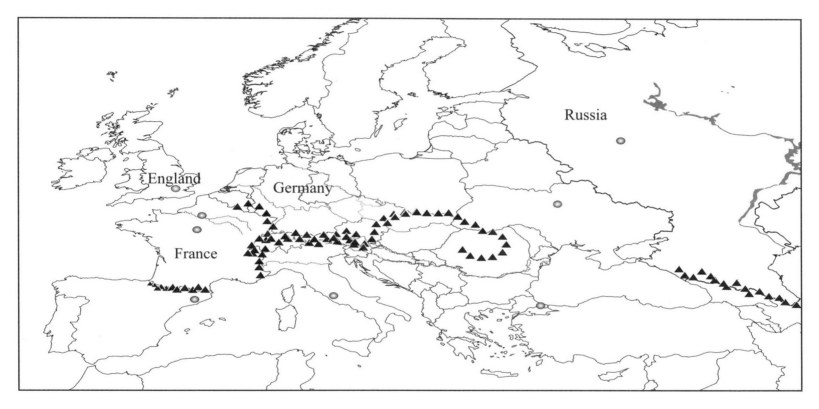

Detail from *Trivium Tables, Geography Cycle 2*.

Try drawing this map in the space below.

Your drawing:

History Notes 15(a) Trace, then write the sentence.

During World War I, Great Britain, France, and Russia were Allies and fought against Austria-Hungary and Germany, which were called the Central Powers. In 1917, the U.S. entered the war, assisting the Allies.

History Note 15(b) Trace, then write the sentence.

During World War I, Great Britain, France, and Russia were Allies and fought against Austria-Hungary and Germany, which were called the Central Powers. In 1917, the U.S. entered the war, assisting the Allies.

Drawing Figures (Review)

Practice drawing figures using the head length to sketch the proportions just as you did in the Joan of Arc drawing (see page 30).

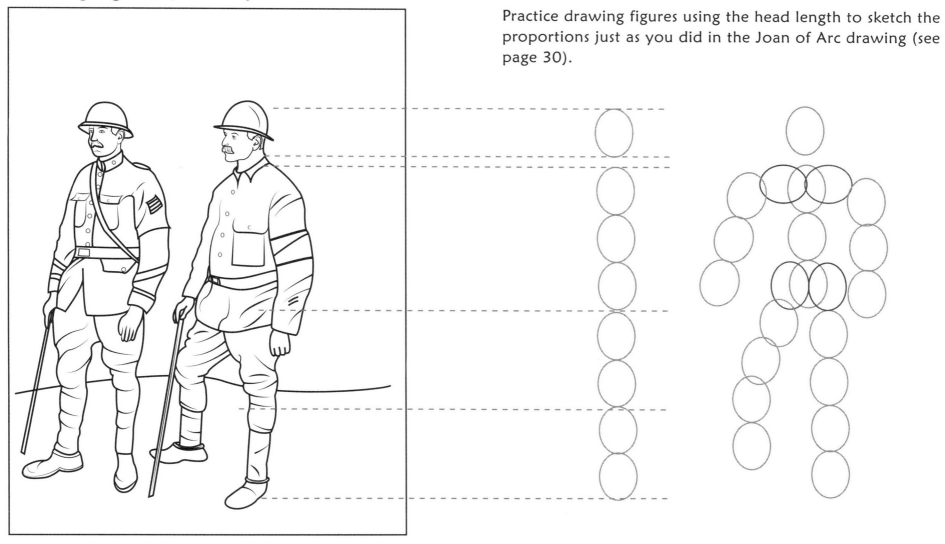

Belgian policeman and French policeman during World War I

Your drawing:

History Note 16(a) Trace, then write the sentence.

World War II began in 1939 when Hitler invaded Poland.

Two engagements that helped the U.S. win the Pacific

front were the Battle of Midway and dropping atomic

bombs on Hiroshima and Nagasaki in 1945.

History Note 16(b) Trace, then write the sentence.

World War II began in 1939 when Hitler invaded Poland.

Two engagements that helped the U.S. win the Pacific

front were the Battle of Midway and dropping atomic

bombs on Hiroshima and Nagasaki in 1945.

Blending

USS *Bunker Hill* at Okinawa

This illustration was drawn from a photo taken at the Battle of Okinawa (Japan), during WWII. The USS *Bunker Hill* had just been hit by two *kamikazes** within 30 seconds. The explosions caused the towering black mountain of smoke.

In order to draw black smoke like this, or thunder clouds, you can use a soft pencil (number 2 or HB). Lean the pencil almost all the way over to the side and rub it in circles to create the billows you see in the picture.

Then, **blend** the pencil shading. You can use your finger, a Q-tip, or a blending tool such as a "stompy" or "blending stump," which can be bought at an art or craft store.

Take your blending tool and rub it in circles to create the effects you like. It may take some practice to discover how to get the effect you want.

If you want to lighten an area, use an eraser and rub in light circles.

Try drawing this scene or a cloudy sky, using blending.

*Kamikaze means a suicidal attack by a WWII Japanese pilot in an airplane loaded with explosives.

Your drawing:

History Note 17(a) Trace, then write the sentence.

World War II Axis leaders were: Hitler of Germany, Tojo of Japan, and Mussolini of Italy. World War II Ally leaders were: Churchill of England, Roosevelt, Eisenhower, and MacArthur of the U.S., and Stalin of the U.S.S.R.

History Note 17(b) Trace, then write the sentence.

World War II Axis leaders were: Hitler of Germany, Tojo of Japan, and Mussolini of Italy. World War II Ally leaders were: Churchill of England, Roosevelt, Eisenhower, and MacArthur of the U.S., and Stalin of the U.S.S.R.

Profile

Josef Stalin

This portrait of Josef Stalin is drawn in **profile**, which means in a side view, rather than straight on.

Some artists draw a profile by having their subject sit near a wall and tracing the shadow their profile casts. You could try this by having someone sit near a wall. Tape your paper to the wall, and place a bright lamp on the other side of your subject. Adjust the distance of the lamp until it casts a shadow with a sharp line. Then trace the profile.

Remove your paper from the wall and look at your subject to draw in their eye, ear, hairline, and other details.

Try drawing this profile of Stalin or try the shadow method.

Your drawing:

History Note 18(a) Trace, then write the sentence.

In 1945, after the League of Nations failed to prevent World War II, American President Roosevelt, British Prime Minister Churchill, and U.S.S.R. Premier Stalin began the United Nations.

History Note 18(b) Trace, then write the sentence.

In 1945, after the League of Nations failed to prevent World War II, American President Roosevelt, British Prime Minister Churchill, and U.S.S.R. Premier Stalin began the United Nations.

The Modern Movement

United Nations Headquarters, New York City, New York

This building is the United Nations headquarters in New York City. Like many tall buildings, it was designed in the style of the **Modern Movement**. This was a trend that began after World War II, in which artists and architects wanted a "new" look. They did not want to use anything that looked historical. They did not want to use columns from ancient Greece, for example, on this building. They wanted to use new materials, such as mirrored glass and concrete, instead of wood or stone. They wanted everything to be useful and nothing that was solely decorative. This resulted in buildings like this one at the left. It looms tall and powerful over the area like a monolith, with no reminders of the past. The only design element is the pattern in the repetition of windows in straight lines and in the repetition of flags in front.

Try drawing this building. You might want to use a ruler to make the lines straight and smooth.

Your drawing:

History Note 13(c) Review. Trace, then write the sentence.

Watt's steam engine, Cartwright's power loom,

and Whitney's cotton gin spurred the Industrial

Revolution that began in the 1760s.

History Note 14(c) Review. Trace, then write the sentence.

Clemenceau of France, Lloyd George of England,

Nicholas II of Russia, Wilhelm II of Germany, and

Wilson of the U.S. were leaders during World War I,

which started in 1914 and ended in 1918.

History Sentence 15(c) Review. Trace, then write the sentence.

During World War I, Great Britain, France, and Russia were Allies and fought against Austria-Hungary and Germany, which were called the Central Powers. In 1917, the U.S. entered the war, assisting the Allies.

In this space, draw one of the art lessons again for practice.

History Sentence 16(c) Review. Trace, then write the sentence.

World War II began in 1939 when Hitler invaded Poland.

Two engagements that helped the U.S. win the Pacific

front were the Battle of Midway and dropping atomic

bombs on Hiroshima and Nagasaki in 1945.

History Note 17(c) Review. Trace, then write the sentence.

World War II Axis leaders were: Hitler of Germany, Tojo of Japan, and Mussolini of Italy. World War II Ally leaders were: Churchill of England, Roosevelt, Eisenhower, and MacArthur of the U.S., and Stalin of the U.S.S.R.

History Note 18(c) Review. Trace, then write the sentence.

In 1945, after the League of Nations failed to prevent World War II, American President Roosevelt, British Prime Minister Churchill, and U.S.S.R. Premier Stalin began the United Nations.

For practice, draw one of the art lessons again in this space.

History Note 19(a) Trace, then write the sentence.

In 1950, General Douglas MacArthur led U.N. troops to stop communist North Korea from capturing all of South Korea during the Korean War.

History Note 19(b) Trace, then write the sentence.

In 1950, General Douglas MacArthur led U.N. troops to stop communist North Korea from capturing all of South Korea during the Korean War.

Overlapping

Korean girl carrying brother in Haengju, Korea

This illustration was made from a photograph of a Korean girl carrying her brother. Notice that there is a huge military tank in the background. This tells us this is a story about children during war time.

The technique that gives this picture depth is called **overlapping**. The children overlap the tank. You can see part of the tank on the right and part of it on the left. Our brains know that there is one whole tank in the background, not just part of one on one side and part of another on the other side, even though that is all that is drawn. Our brains are able to fill in the missing information.

The tank overlaps a hill, too. Do you see the hill behind the tank on the right side? That is another clue to the composition. It gives the picture a lot of depth.

Try drawing this scene. Play close attention to lining up the sides of the tank. You might even want to draw the entire tank first (very lightly with a hard pencil) then erase the portion where the children will go. Then draw the children in. If the lines of the tank do not match up, the illusion will not work.

Your drawing:

History Note 20(a) Trace, then write the sentence.

In 1965, President Johnson sent U.S. troops to

stop communist North Vietnam from capturing

all of South Vietnam during the Vietnam War.

History Note 20(b) Trace, then write the sentence.

In 1965, President Johnson sent U.S. troops to stop communist North Vietnam from capturing all of South Vietnam during the Vietnam War.

Camouflage

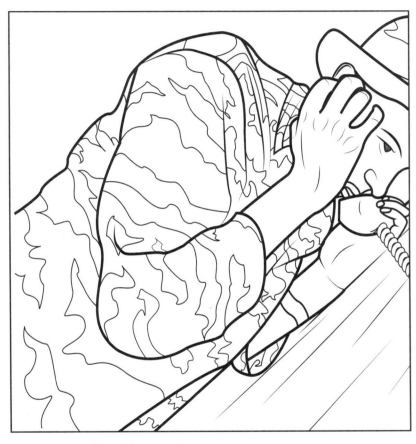

U.S. soldier of the Vietnam War

The soldier in this drawing is wearing **camouflage**. If you have studied animals, you know that animals' stripes make them harder to see. U.S. soldiers who went to Vietnam used the same idea to make themselves less visible in the jungle.

At the beginning of the Vietnam War, soldiers wore solid green uniforms which made them a little harder to see. By the end of the Vietnam War, they had switched to the tiger striped pattern you see in this picture, which was printed with green, dark brown, and tan stripes.

Artists and scientists both worked on developing the best camouflage design to make soldiers hard to see.

Today, camouflage has a computer generated look, made up of squares, and has been designed for different environments from jungle to desert.

Try drawing this scene, concentrating on the camouflage pattern in the uniform.

Your drawing:

History Note 21(a) Trace, then write the sentence.

In the 1980s, British Prime Minister Margaret Thatcher and U.S. President Ronald Reagan worked together to end the Cold War, lessen big government, and strengthen the conservative movement.

History Note 21(b) Trace, then write the sentence.

In the 1980s, British Prime Minister Margaret Thatcher and U.S. President Ronald Reagan worked together to end the Cold War, lessen big government, and strengthen the conservative movement.

Showing Motion

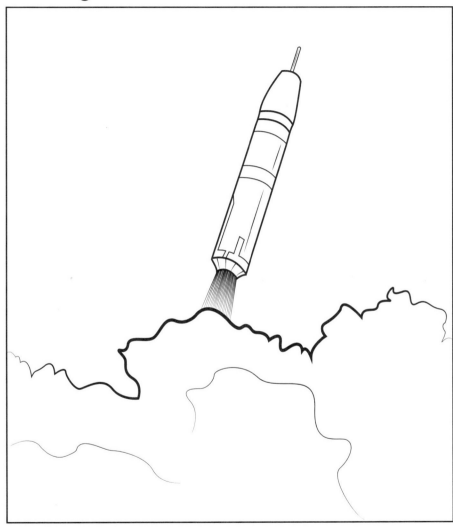

First launch of a Trident missile

This illustration clearly shows a missile in motion. It has just blasted off and is headed up toward space. How do we know that? There are several clues that work together to **show motion**. First, the position of the rocket is important. It is in the air and is at an angle. You also see lines of fire shooting from the end.

Even though this illustration is not moving, our brains interpret these clues so that we know the rocket ship is moving.

The lines just under the missile also help to show where the missile has been and where it is going.

Try drawing this missile in motion. Pay close attention to the lines of the rocket and the fire.

Use your finger, a cotton swab, or a blending tool to smudge the billowing smoke.

Your drawing:

History Note 22(a) Trace, then write the sentence.

In 1989, communist dictators began to fall in Eastern Europe when Soviet President Gorbachev refused to back them up with military force.

History Note 22(b) Trace, then write the sentence.

In 1989, communist dictators began to fall in Eastern Europe when Soviet President Gorbachev refused to back them up with military force.

Graffiti

Graffiti from the Berlin Wall

At the end of World War II, Germany was divided into four zones, each occupied by either the United States, Great Britain, France, or Russia. Russia established communist rule over its area, East Germany. People in that area began to move into the other areas where there was more freedom. The communists decided to build a wall to keep people from leaving East Germany.

The wall was built in one night, surprising everyone. It was hundreds of miles long, cutting through Berlin (the capital city) and surrounding all of East Germany.

Twenty-nine years later, communism began to fall, and the East German government announced that its borders were open. People on both sides of the wall began to chip away at it and tore most of it down themselves. East and West Germany became one country again in 1990.

The sides of the wall facing West Germany had been covered with **graffiti**, which describes any painting or drawing on public property that has not been commissioned. People often expressed their longing for freedom on the wall.

These illustrations can still be seen on a portion of the Berlin Wall that was left standing. Try drawing these figures, or draw the graffiti you would paint if there were such a wall near you.

Your drawing:

History Note 23(a) Trace, then write the sentence.

In 1990, President Bush sent troops to the Persian Gulf to expel Iraqi leader Saddam Hussein from Kuwait during the Gulf War.

History Note 23(b) Trace, then write the sentence.

In 1990, President Bush sent troops to the Persian Gulf to expel Iraqi leader Saddam Hussein from Kuwait during the Gulf War.

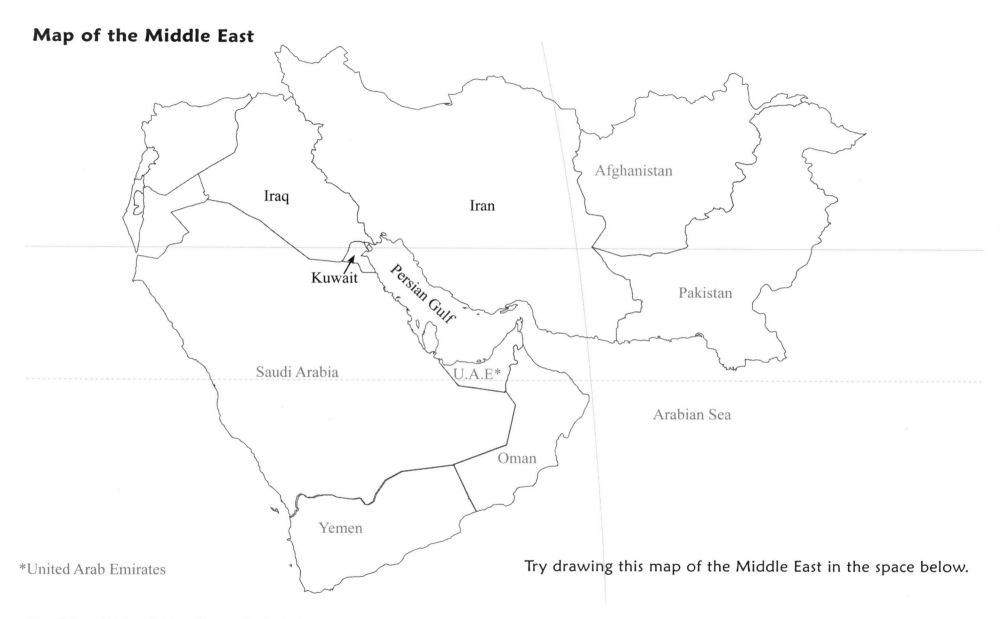

Your drawing:

History Note 24(a) Trace, then write the sentence.

In 1994, South African President de Klerk allowed free elections. Nelson Mandela became the first black president, demonstrating apartheid was ending.

History Note 24(b) Trace, then write the sentence.

In 1994, South African President de Klerk allowed free elections. Nelson Mandela became the first black president, demonstrating apartheid was ending.

Portraiture

Nelson Mandela in Johannesburg, Gauteng

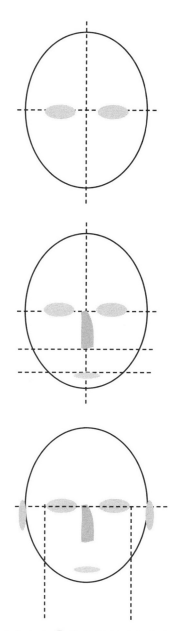

A **portrait** is a drawing of just a person's head. Start by lightly drawing some guidelines.

1) Draw an oval, then lightly sketch a verticle straight line through the oval.
2) Draw a straight horizontal line in the middle of the oval.
3) Sketch in two ovals right on the line where eyes will go.
4) Midway between the horizontal line and the base of the oval, draw a second horizontal line.
5) This second line will be where the bottom of the nose will go.
6) Draw in the nose from between the eyes to the second straight line.
7) Draw a third horizontal line midway between the second line and the bottom of the oval. This third line will be where the lips meet.
8) Draw the lips on the third line.
9) Sketch in the hairline, which can cover half or most of the forehead. (The top of the oval is the very top of the head.)
10) Draw dotted lines straight down from the outside of the eyes. These indicate where the neck will be.
11) Ears will begin above the eye line and extend almost to the nose line.
12) Look carefully at the photo to draw in details such as eyebrows and facial lines.

Your drawing:

History Note 19(c) Review. Trace, then write the sentence.

In 1950, General Douglas MacArthur led U.N. troops to stop communist North Korea from capturing all of South Korea during the Korean War.

History Note 20(c) Review. Trace, then write the sentence.

In 1965, President Johnson sent U.S. troops to stop communist North Vietnam from capturing all of South Vietnam during the Vietnam War.

History Note 21(c) Review. Trace, then write the sentence.

In the 1980s, British Prime Minister Margaret Thatcher and U.S. President Ronald Reagan worked together to end the Cold War, lessen big government, and strengthen the conservative movement.

For practice, draw one of the art lessons again in this space.

History Note 22(c) Review. Trace, then write the sentence.

In 1989, communist dictators began to fall in Eastern Europe when Soviet President Gorbachev refused to back them up with military force.

History Note 23(c) Review. Trace, then write the sentence.

In 1990, President Bush sent troops to the Persian Gulf to expel Iraqi leader Saddam Hussein from Kuwait during the Gulf War.

History Note 24(c) Review. Trace, then write the sentence.

In 1994, South African President de Klerk allowed free elections. Nelson Mandela became the first black president, demonstrating apartheid was ending.

For practice, draw one of the art lessons again in this space.

For practice, draw one of the art lessons again in this space.

For practice, draw one of the art lessons again in this space.

For practice, draw one of the art lessons again in this space.

For practice, draw one of the art lessons again in this space.

For practice, draw one of the art lessons again in this space.

Image Credits

These coloring illustrations are a rendering of a photograph, piece of artwork, or a public domain image that represents an important historical event or person from medieval to modern world history. Most drawings represent a memory peg image from Classical Conversations® MultiMedia Classical Acts & Facts™ History Cards. (The corresponding history card number and title is indicated in parentheses.)

Page	10	Detail of a miniature of Charlemagne being crowned emperor, *Chroniques de France ou St. Denis* (#65 Charlemagne Crowned Emperor of Europe) Shown also on pages 11 and 14
Page	18	Basilica roof, Florence, Italy (#70 East-West Schism of the Church)
Page	18	Eastern-Orthodox cupola, Russia (#70 East-West Schism of the Church)
Page	22	*The Nándorfehérvár Battle*, artist unknown (#72 The Crusades)
Page	26	*King John Signs the Magna Carta*, James W. E. Doyle (#79 England's Magna Carta)
Page	30	*Jeanne D'Arc at the Siege of Orléans*, Jules-Eugène Lenepveu (#82 The Hundred Years' War and Black Death)
Page	34	Leonardo da Vinci's sketch of a flying machine (#83 The Renaissance)
Page	46	Detail from New Testament translation by Martin Luther (woodcut) 1525 (#94 Protestant Reformation)
Page	50	Spanish Conquistadors in the Americas, *The Whole Army Knelt in the Mud and Confessed Their Sins*, J. H. Robinson (#95 Spanish Conquistadors in the Americas)
Page	54	Imperial Crown of Austria (#93 Age of Absolute Monarchs)
Page	58	*Ivan the Great Tearing the Khan's Letter to Pieces* (detail), Aleksey D. Kivshenko (#90 Czar Ivan the Great of Russia)
Page	62	*An Execution, Place de la Revolution* (detail), Pierre Antoine de Machy (#110 French Revolution)
Page	66	*Napoleon I on His Imperial Throne*, Jean Auguste Dominique Ingres (#113 Napoleon Crowned Emperor of France)
Page	78	Steam Locomotive (#106 Age of Industry)
Page	86	Belgian policeman and French policeman, World War I Document Archive (#136 World War I and President Wilson)
Page	90	USS *Bunker Hill* at Okinawa, Tony Faccone, Archival Research Catalog, U.S. National Archives (#141 World War II and President Franklin D. Roosevelt)
Page	94	Josef Stalin, Library of Congress, LC-USW33-019081-C (#142 Stalin of the USSR and the Katyn Massacre)
Page	98	United Nations Headquarters, Jeremy Edwards (#143 The United Nations Formed)
Page	110	Korean girl carrying brother in Haengju, Korea, Air Force Major R. V. Spencer (#149 The Korean War)
Page	114	U.S. Soldier of the Vietnam War, "Soldier firing M-16 while another calls for support," (#153 The Vietnam War)
Page	118	First launch of a Trident missile (#144 The Cold War)
Page	122	Graffiti from the Berlin Wall, Action Press (#157 Fall of Communism in Eastern Europe)
Page	130	Nelson Mandela in Johannesburg, Gaugeng (#159 Apartheid Abolished in South Africa) South Africa The Good News. "Nelson Mandela in Johannesburg, Gauteng, on 13 May 1998." Creative Commons, 13 May 2008. Web. 26 Nov. 2011.<http://en.wikipedia.org/wiki/File:Nelson_Mandela-2008_%28edit%29.jpg>.

Additional products from

Classical Christian Education... Made Approachable

As a modern parent, are you intimidated at the prospect of building a classical, Christian education for your family? Let this booklet show you a blueprint for the tools of learning! Learn how you too can build your family's home-centered, classical education using the building blocks of knowledge, understanding, and wisdom.

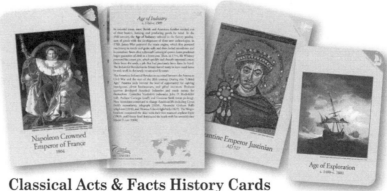

Classical Acts & Facts History Cards

Classical Conversations has developed its own timeline of 161 historical events, representing major cultures on every continent. The events are divided into seven ages and produced as cards similar to our Classical Acts & Facts Science Cards, with the event title on the front and a fuller description of the event on the back. Each card front also contains a beautiful memory peg image. Images were chosen to serve families all the way through cultural studies in the upper levels of Challenge. The back of each card also includes a world map, pinpointing the event location, and a general timeline, illustrating when the event occurred relative to known history.